MW01342316

Signs & Symbols of our Ancestors

an illustrated collection of sacred stories

edited by

Natalia Zukerman & Lisa Ferraro

illustrations by Natalia Zukerman

Artwork by Natalia Zukerman
Book design by Liz Kalloch.
Author photo by Sandy Morris.

Armature Publishing
c/o Lisa Ferraro
PO Box 254
Worthington, OH 43085
soulcallglobal.org
info@soulcallglobal.org

Contents

Introduction

Natalia Zukerman & Lisa Ferraro

"For the Homeric Greeks, *kleos,* fame, was made of song. Vibrations in air contained the measure and memory of a person's life.

To listen was therefore to learn what endures.

I turned my ear to trees, seeking ecological kleos. I found no heroes, no individuals around whom history pivots. Instead, living memories of trees, manifest in their songs, tell of life's community, a net of relations. We humans belong within this conversation, as blood kin and incarnate members. To listen is therefore to hear our voices and those of our family.

To listen is therefore to touch a stethoscope to the skin of a landscape, to hear what stirs below."

–David George Haskell,
The Songs of Trees: Stories from Nature's Great Connectors

Given the space and permission, we all have the ability to experience many dimensions of existence. We compiled these sacred stories not only as permission, but as invitations to listen

more deeply to Spirit, to plants, to animals, to the ancestors that we know of, the ancestors we don't, and even our future generations.

It has been an honor to collect these stories and bring these images to life. Our great hope is that these pages awaken a recognition in you that you indeed are a conduit for dreams, for songs, for birds, for flowers, a shooting star, a tug of your sheet, a flickering light, footsteps, a creaking door, a tap on the wall, a fox running across newly fallen snow. Use these pages as you would a deck of spirit cards and open to the conversations, the songs awaiting the singer, the air itself inviting and inventing the stories not yet told.

—Natalia Zukerman & Lisa Ferraro

The Next Hello

Billie Gray

November 9th, 1967 was the happiest day of my life. My son, Timothy Clarence Gray, the most beautiful, amazing human being, came to planet Earth that day. The joy my heart experienced was indescribable.

Tim was a loving, kind, and brilliant person. The bond between us was so strong. I raised him as a single mom and he was my only child. Tim made me proud in so many ways. He was a Morehouse graduate, an Emory University MBA recipient, but more than anything else, he was an exceptionally caring and loving person who enjoyed life to the fullest each day.

June 14th, 2016, was the saddest, most traumatic day of my life. Tim died from a rare blood clotting disorder which first started in 2000. As his illness became progressively worse, he battled for as long and as hard as he could.

Tim's death left me a member of a club that no one wants to join: the grieving mother's club. I spent much of my time over a long period in shock and deep grief. I missed Tim so much. I wanted to feel his presence again. I wanted to talk to him, touch him, but most of all I wanted to hug him so tightly. I just couldn't

Tim came and sat beside me. He was so real that I felt I could touch and hug him. I felt like I was in the twilight zone. My heart started to race. I thought I would faint.

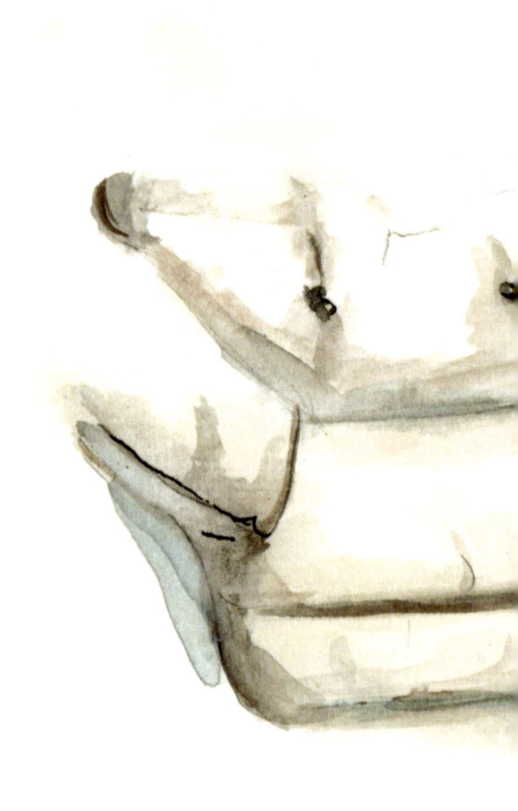

believe that this would never be possible again. I began making attempts at connecting with Tim, but was never successful. I talked to other parents whose children had died and they spoke of often feeling the presence of their deceased children. I joined the Compassionate Friends Organization. Many parents in that

organization also talked about various kinds of connections they made with their deceased children. Why couldn't I connect with my son? We had a love that should be able to transcend the perceived barriers of dimensions. What was wrong with me? Why couldn't I make a connection with my sweet Tim?

I started making the rounds to a few psychics and clairvoyants, but the attempts to contact Tim were still unsuccessful. I also started psychotherapy and the therapist assured me that when I was ready, the connection would happen.

May, 2020, in my boredom and isolation during the COVID-19 Pandemic, I decided to start taking classes on Zoom. One of the classes that I was guided to take was on the poet Rumi. The instructor was Lisa Ferraro. At our first class meeting, she did a meditation with us where she asked us to call forth someone who had gone to another dimension. I was seated on my sofa listening to the meditation on my iPad, and, as I closed my eyes, Tim came and sat beside me. He was so real that I felt I could touch and hug him. I felt like I was in the twilight zone. My heart started to race. I thought I would faint. I kept my eyes closed for fear that if I opened them, I would lose Tim again. I didn't hear anything else Lisa was saying. As I came out of the meditation, I no longer felt fear but rather a sense of peace and joy. I had finally made a connection with my Tim!

That was the beginning of many more connections to come: when I am watching sports; when I lose something and I hear his voice say, “Look over there”; when celebrating my birthday. Now when the pain of missing him in physical form becomes so great, I can connect with his presence and hear his voice telling me he is here. I now welcome rather than fear his presence.

The reader of this story may ask why it took so long for my connection with Tim to happen. I would say it was fear of having to say goodbye over and over again. I thought that would be unbearable. Once this connection was made, I learned it wasn’t unbearable because I now know with the next goodbye, there will also be the next hello. I have learned to embrace and cherish both.

Trying to process divinity
with anything other than
a heart just makes it small.

The Hum of Wings

Kate Mapother

I'm learning to fly, but I ain't got wings.
Coming down is the hardest thing.
—"Learning to Fly" by Tom Petty and the Heartbreakers

In spring of 2017, the pain of my nephew, David's death had its heel in my solar plexus. He'd been dead less than a month. What was left of me wasn't much more than shallow breath and a deep ache. With so much of his heart still in the world, I couldn't fathom how he wasn't physically here anymore. How does a light like his just go out? And what was I to do now with the furious love echoing through my paper-thin veins?

I went to Arizona for his memorial – to the desert where we'd grown up like siblings. I hadn't been back in ten years. June had the southwest in a choke-hold of record-breaking temperatures. I got off the plane in Tucson, and stepped into a diorama of my insides, everything parched and brittle. A match-strike from an inferno.

In the early mornings before anyone else was up, I'd sit in my sister's swimming pool. That's where I was the first time he came to me. Heart sinking, body floating in lukewarm water at five in the morning, writing his eulogy in my head. I heard the hum of wings, looked up and made eye contact with half an ounce of flying god. The weight of a soul perhaps. He wasn't a foot from my face, hovering above the water, his tiny head cocked sideways. He bobbed there for a couple seconds before racing back to the mesquite trees. He perched himself on a low branch, and watched me for an hour or so.

Later that morning I said to my sister, "You have a really cool hummingbird in your yard."

"No," she said. "We don't get any here. I've tried for years to attract them, but they don't come."

"Well," I said, "You've got one now." We looked at one another for a moment. Then she said the quiet part out loud: "I think it's him, sissy."

It felt like him, like a spark of his love still in the world, but it was silly to think a bird was the soul of a person, wasn't it? When she said those words though, I remembered that God made fireflies and thunderbolts. Who was I to question the ways light comes into this world?

At his memorial, I gave his eulogy. The tiny, ruby-throated bird flew in under the rental tent, circling my head so fast, I never saw him until we played back the video after the service. He appeared while I spoke and while David's brother spoke. The three amigos. He was completing the circuitry of us, once again.

At the reception, the caterer approached my sister and whispered there was something happening outside the room where they had set up. "You should come see this," she said.

My sister and I went back to find him on the ground, right outside the glass door. "He's been there a while," the caterer said, "just sitting on the ground. I thought he was dead or hurt, but every now and again he hovers up and looks in. I've never seen a hummingbird do that." He saw my sister and I through the glass, flew up and hung there for a second, like he wanted to make sure we knew he was there. Then he raced off to the trees.

The day I left my sisters to go back to New York, I was in the guest house. My bags were packed but it was too early to leave for the airport. The front door was open, and I was reading on the couch when I heard the flutter of his break-neck wings. He was before me again, suspended in that fierce and weightless grace. He stared at me for several seconds, then darted back out the door. I swear it put actual voltage in my chest, like he was trying to jump-start my broken heart. That was the kind of man he was in life. The kind that came to your rescue for no reason other than it pained him to see anyone hurting. At his memorial, friends recounted story after story of his empathy and kindness. He was a gorgeous human being, a heart like a sky.

A year after he died, hummingbird-Dave brought a friend to my sister's yard. She laid little jelly-bean eggs in a nest the size of a ping pong ball in the spider plant near the pool. They come back every year now. He comes to me in flight almost everywhere, so close I hear him before I see him. He's been with me in canyons where hummingbirds aren't known to be. Once, we hung out together in an old desert cantina. He flew in under the canopy and played over my head while I drank a beer. My grief is suspended in these moments of divine encounter. They've become welcome pauses in the crushing weight of his death; places I can catch my breath, even if for just a minute or two.

I stopped being surprised by his visits, but never stopped being in awe of them. Never lost the physical feeling of sacred connection to some energy beyond what I could understand with my mind. Losing David and finding him again this way taught me that some things are meant to stay embodied. Trying to process divinity with anything other than a heart just makes it small. When he comes around, I let myself be astonished, let these merciful little miracles wash me clean.

In the mid-80's, Tom Petty and the Heartbreakers filmed the video for the song "Learning to Fly" in Arizona. David auditioned and got the part of a young man in a desert cantina having an out-of-body experience, while Tom sings about learning to fly without wings; about coming down being the hardest thing. The song became a family anthem. To us, it was David's song, his video. When I watch it now, it feels prescient.

When Tom Petty died, just five months after David, it was another shocking loss. It was early October and I was deep in the woods of upstate New York with my dog, a place I didn't usually get cell service. My phone beeped. It was a news alert: "Tom Petty, dead at 66," it said.

I sat down by a pond and cried. I didn't hear the familiar hum of wings; David made no appearance. The only sound was the dog rooting through the leaves. I sat for a while then wiped my face and stood to go, and there in the water before me were two massive oak trees, fallen into the shape of a cross. Their mossy, watery branches fanned out. Just like wings.

I smiled at the thought of the two of them somewhere together, all flight and song, the hard things finally over.

Feathers from Puppie

Dominique Sacco

As the first of twelve grandchildren, my grandfather ("Puppie" as I called him), meant so much to me. He wasn't an overly affectionate man in the traditional sense; you knew he loved you by the way he laughed with you. He appreciated the simple things in life and found the humor in it all. The many fond memories I have of him leave me with bittersweet laughter.

As a child of divorced parents, I spent a lot of time at the home of my maternal grandparents. Puppie became the father figure in my life. He always made me feel a sense of belonging. He made me feel as if I was one of his own children.

The day of Puppie's funeral, November 30th, 2006, is a day which will forever be etched into my heart. At the cemetery, we had a dove releasing ceremony during which several doves

were released into the air to fly off together. Then there was one white dove which was the representation of Puppie. Each of his five children and his wife, my Nunnie, received a white feather, presumably from this white dove, as an acknowledgment of the significant relationship and bond between father and children, husband and wife. When asked how many children he had, the dove keeper was told five even though I was always considered the sixth child. I did not receive a feather. I understood this, but still felt the smallest ache in my heart because I wanted a feather.

No less than 150 mourners huddled together under the gray November sky as the crisp winds chilled us to the bone. As I stood sobbing with my head hung down and my arms loosely crossed against my chest, the dove keeper released the dove representing Puppie into the air. All eyes were on that lone white dove as it began to fly off and join the others. As he flew up through the lightly falling snow, a long white feather separated from one of his wings and began to float down, down, down, careening toward the group as all watched on! The younger children were jumping and taking swipes at it in an effort to have a feather from Puppie! My head was still hanging with sadness as I felt something soft slide into my half-opened left fist. The feather! The feather had made its way, almost willfully, into my hand. I felt immediate peace in that moment. The spirit as Puppie affirming me as the sixth child in his funny way!

He appreciated the simple things in life and found the humor in it all. The many fond memories I have of him leave me with bittersweet laughter.

The spirit as Puppie continues to show up as a white feather anytime I feel I need a little encouragement or a lift during trying times.

She Made It After All

Christie Hardwick

My mother loved the movie *Out of Africa*. She had always wanted to see the vast expanse of the Serengeti. She wanted to witness a dazzle of zebra, a pack of elephants, or the magnificence of a pride of lions.

She loved the idea of a woman on her own, resilient, courageous, without a brood of children wearing her down. The movie *Out of Africa* came out after she'd raised seven children. We were all alive and no one was in jail (she always joked that this was the measure of success for a parent).

She worked hard to keep us safe and fed and to give us possibilities. I didn't appreciate it for many years, but I do now. I was the last of her children to speak with her after 80 years on the planet. She wasn't scheduled to die that day, the day after I saw her, but she did.

It was near Valentine's Day, so my wife and I brought her a balloon and a plant for her room in the rehab facility. She had trouble walking because she was obese and stationary for too long. She had no machines attached to her, no oxygen or other life support. She just lay propped up, giving audience. She shared stories of her childhood which made clear that my romantic version of her marriage at age 16 was a fairy tale. Her mother kicked her out when she was pregnant with her first child. I had always imagined that her mother was so sad her daughter was running away with the tall, dark, and handsome Air Force man. Instead, my mother said, "She packed my bag! I didn't want to go!" She went further back in time and reminisced about her neighborhood school, PS 33 in Buffalo, New York.

I shared our annual picture book with her to catch her up on my life. She listened to my descriptions of each picture, our domestic and international travels, our beautiful homes. After I turned the last page, she smiled, saying, "What a dynamic couple." I told her we needed to leave and that we would be back. She said simply, "You are dismissed."

When she was found non-responsive a day later, I was shocked. Only then did I understand her talk with us was a review of her life. She was complete.

We had mother cremated and, per her wishes, took her ashes out in a boat on the San Francisco Bay. As we poured her remains into the choppy, gray water, we played the theme song from *Out of Africa*. A sound overwhelmed the music. We looked up to see a biplane fly over the boat and above the bridge.

My mother's favorite scene in the movie was when the character played by Robert Redford takes Meryl Streep over the Serengeti in his biplane. We, her children, all thought it was auspicious and asked around about a biplane's probability in the area. Folks could not remember seeing a biplane over the San Francisco Bay before. I knew it was her.

I went to Africa the same year and climbed up 200 steps to a vista point in Johannesburg. Jane played the theme from *Out of Africa* on her phone, saying, "We can send mom a message that you made it here." I took a deep breath, reveling in the expansive view. At that moment, a biplane flew directly into the scene. My wife exclaimed, "It's your mom! She's here!" As my tears touched down, I quietly said to myself, "Yes. She made it to Africa after all."

She loved the idea
of a woman on her own,
resilient, courageous,
without a brood
of children
wearing her down.

DURACELL

Batteries

Care Gerdeman

Shortly after my husband Dave transitioned, maybe two weeks, I was home by myself for the first time since he left. I was exhausted and lying on the sofa with my eyes closed. I was listening to *The Daily Show*: "Rally to Restore Sanity," in Washington DC. Dave wanted to go to that and had even checked into chartering a bus to take a group of people from North Carolina to the rally.

Dave loved electronic gadgets. He collected them. While I was lying there, a timer/thermometer "thingy" went off in the kitchen. It was one of his and I had not moved it from the counter. It was the first time it had gone off since he had been gone. It felt like he had walked in from the garage through the kitchen and was standing just a few feet away from me. He asked me if I was too tired to get up and turn off the alarm. I answered, "Yes." He asked

if I would like him to turn it off and I answered, "Yes." It stopped buzzing immediately. I did not move or look at this gadget for at least a week after that. When I did pick it up to move it, I realized it had no batteries in it.

A couple of months later I was at my brother's house in Key West with our daughter, Carly. We had not had time to grieve together at the time of Dave's passing. The first night there, sitting on the patio overlooking the Gulf of Mexico, we drank beer and told Dave stories. Suddenly one of the beer bottles on the table started to whistle. This is something Dave did often. He would blow into whatever bottle he had and make it whistle. There was a sea breeze, but there were other bottles on the table too, and none of them were whistling. The whistling continued over several hours. It was the kind of evening he would have enjoyed so much, and he still seemed to be that night.

Also on that trip, our other daughter Paula called in tears saying she had received a call from her dad's phone. She picked it up and his message played. I had his phone with me and there were no outgoing calls. Her phone also showed no incoming or outgoing calls.

I have felt Dave's presence often, especially in the house we built together in North Carolina. Ten years later I can still feel him sometimes. It is a comforting feeling. It is the feeling that we are all connected and part of Source. When I am open and present, the door is open to the universe and I can feel that connection. I have felt sad and felt the loss, but I have never felt alone.

One or two days after he passed, I was leaving the house for the first time with our daughters and my sister to make arrangements at the funeral home. As we pulled out of the driveway, two deer came out of the woods and ran alongside the car for a while. A year later, on Dave's birthday, I had the same experience of two deer coming out of the woods and running alongside the car.

There is always a divine presence with us. It is part of us whether we recognize it or not.

When I am open
and present,
the door is open
to the universe
and I can feel
that connection.

Essence

Marie Martini

Sometimes all I need to do is pause and listen, opening my awareness to the subtle messages from animal spirit and nature. This allows me to connect with the energy and guidance of the ancestors. I often have an experience of this when I find myself at a crossroads in life, or when I'm moving in a new direction.

My grandmother had determination, willpower, and was always steadfast in accomplishing her goals. A wise teacher and friend, I have always been proud of her feminine power as well as her masculine strength. Born in 1926, she had to adapt at age 14 after her mother passed. She was left to help raise her siblings as the oldest child. Against the odds, she went on to earn a degree in both engineering and architectural drafting, not common for women in the late 40's, early 50's. Her resolve and grit saw her through. She refused to conform. This relentless passion led her to meet my grandfather and raise seven children. Their loyalty survived through many ups and downs. They were married for 70 years.

I was hiking across ocean-view trails surrounded by the vast sand dunes of Cape Cod National Seashore as the sun began to set. My partner and I tread up and over a long causeway connecting the solitude of the beach and Race Point Lighthouse. The late January air was cold and the wind picked up, but we stopped to feel the warmth of the sun on our faces. When I looked up, a red fox was trotting down the path, heading right for us. We stood still, in fascination of this beautiful, wild creature. It looked us dead in the eyes, showing no fear or judgment, only confidence and natural charisma as it sauntered onward, along its hunt for an evening meal.

I felt my grandmother speaking to me that evening, reminding me to trust my instincts and let go of the past, to move forward into tomorrow. I was feeling out of balance, unsure of my gender, my identity, and how to share it with the world. Instead of feeling insecure or having the need to fit in to be safe, I felt her challenging me to live my own unique truth. An authentic expression.

For me, the fox symbolizes the essence of both the masculine and the feminine, a beautiful mix. The fox represents Pride. Fox adapts well to new situations, is quick to learn, clever, and skillful.

Fox is physically agile, lithe, and resilient. The fox embodies a mystique and prowess that always leaves me in awe and sends chills down my spine.

These qualities are also true of my grandmother.

When I open myself to embracing the signs and symbols in nature, I feel seen and understood in a new way. Communicating with my ancestors through animal spirit allows me to exist in a realm where I feel empowered and supported by their guidance. It awakens my intuition and inspires me to always remain on my inner quest.

I could sense the presence of all those who had come before me and all who have yet to come. My entire being filled with wonder and gratitude for the trees standing in ceremony, welcoming me home.

Grandmother Tree

Amber Darland

Once, I stumbled upon an old cedar tree, burned out and broken from centuries of fire and storm. Curious, I crawled inside her belly, tracing her charcoaled flesh with my fingers. As I spread my arms wide and leaned into her blackened body, sudden tears—familiar—began running down my cheeks. I let her wisdom, resilience, and comfort envelop me. In that moment, her story of survival was both hers and mine. She explained to me my own scars. She held me like a grandmother.

> *If I am quiet enough, especially as I walk these woods, I can feel my ancestors. I can hear them whispering my name.*

Not long ago, I took a solo weekend away looking for escape from the usual hustle of self-employment and family life. I've always had a hard time slowing down, so it was no surprise that even in the serenity of a secluded yurt I found myself fighting the urge to get up and move as soon as I arrived. I threw on my running clothes and drove a few miles up the road to the trailhead of an unfamiliar forest. I hit the start button on my phone and the robotic voice booming "ACTIVITY STARTED" seemed blasphemous as I began logging my steps. I was keenly aware that my running was wasted in such a beautiful place, yet I continued on, eager to feel productive. As I rounded a corner, my legs suddenly turned to lead and a heaviness throughout my entire body was undeniable. I struggled momentarily, thinking I just needed to push through some morning fatigue. Then I heard it: a commanding voice, clear as day, saying, "Go the pace of nature."

It is a gift when Spirit speaks so clearly.

As I slowed to a complete stop, I gathered my senses. A constellation of trees staggered along the path now had my undivided attention. I could feel my feet becoming tethered to the earth, entwined in their roots. I surrendered to standing there, silently seeking their wise council.

What am I doing here? Who am I?

I heard nothing but the sound of a slight breeze making its way through the canopy, and the knocking of a woodpecker somewhere overhead. The knocking – pounding in perfect rhythm

– sounded like a drum, and I smiled. Then I heard my name. Not my given name, but a name that has come to me in the last few years, a name that I am still gathering the courage to claim as my own.

Sometimes we are lucky enough to receive the same message over and over again.

All at once, my body lightened and I stepped forward. Walking slowly and deliberately now, I could feel the love of my grandmothers. I could sense the presence of all those who had come before me and all who have yet to come. My entire being filled with wonder and gratitude for the trees standing in ceremony, welcoming me home.

Recently, while walking through the woods, my 8-year-old daughter reached out to touch a fallen cedar, its softening bark giving way to ferns and fungi. She turned to me and asked, "Mama, what if this tree is Grandma Rose?"

I simply replied, "What if?" Of course, we both knew the answer.

Dream House

Bob Weisenburger Lipetz

Brenda's heart is as big as an ocean. It seemed so unfair to me that she would suffer so many hard knocks. Karl and Brenda got married, sharing their lives together until Brenda came home after a weekend visiting her parents to find him dead from a heart attack. The following years were a blur of struggles and setbacks.

Being a caregiver takes everything you have, all your time, all your strength, all your money. When her father got Guillain-Barré syndrome that paralyzed him, Brenda quit her job to care for the 6'4" former stone mason. After a couple of years, her father recovered enough that Brenda could return to Columbus and start over. Then her mother declined, and again Brenda quit her job to care for her mother through her final days.

When her mother passed, Brenda was tapped out and exhausted. She had put off tending to herself because she didn't have the time or the healthcare. When Brenda finally went to a doctor, she was told she had stage four cancer and needed immediate surgery and intensive treatment.

The post-surgery treatment, chemotherapy, and daily radiation treatments nearly killed her. After weeks of struggling, she wondered whether to just quit and let nature take its course. But she decided that she loved her sister, my wife, and wanted to spend more time with her, so she pushed through it somehow. I've never seen a more heroic effort.

A slow recovery followed. After a couple of years, Brenda had the strength to sell her parent's house and look for an affordable place to live in Columbus near her sister. She could afford a modest house. We had high hopes as we started on the hunt for Brenda's new home and her new life. We soon discovered that affordable housing doesn't exist in Columbus. The houses we looked at either turned out to be rat holes or were in dicey neighborhoods. Any house that was halfway decent was in contract before we could even look at it.

The search dragged on. After more than a year of looking, Brenda was ready to throw in the towel. After Christmas dinner, she went to bed thinking that her dream was over. In frustration, Brenda called out to her late husband, Karl. "Karl," she told him, "I can't do this anymore. I need your help."

The next day we saw a listing and rushed over to see it. It had everything on her wish list: a cape cod with a garage, a fenced-in backyard, hardwood floors, and a formal dining room. It was just adorable. We rushed in an offer and heard that two other offers had also been placed.

The next day, Brenda got the news that her offer had been accepted, the best Christmas present ever, and to Brenda it was abundantly clear that she had had celestial help. The address of her dream house, the one she had asked her late husband to help her get, of all places, was Karl Street.

We had high hopes as we started on the hunt for Brenda's new home and her new life.

The Thin Place

Deirdre Michael

There is a Celtic term, "thin place," which refers to a place where the barrier between heaven and earth is permeable, malleable, and gossamer-thin, like a veil. Sometimes a loved one can step through the veil and make their presence known. You feel a density, a loving weight. Your soul becomes infused with familiarity, a sense of home.

My grandmother Peggy was born in New York City to Irish immigrants. She often told me stories of how her father would wax eloquent about his hometown Ballyduff along the Wild Atlantic Way in County Kerry. He said there were no finer sunsets, when the sun sank into the sea amid flares of rich hues of crimson and azure.

My grandmother and I chased the sunrise together when I visited her at home on Cape Ann in Massachusetts. We'd wake up early, grab coffee and granola bars, and drive out to Rockport to watch the sunrise from the beach. We'd discuss books, music, news—or nothing. Sitting in companionable silence was just as harmonious.

It was November, 1994, and I was at work when I got the news that she had passed through the veil. I jumped in my car, crying, to drive home to my family. Along the way, there was a wide field, a vast expanse of fallow earth. It was an overcast day, with gray, leaden clouds that obscured the sun. As I drove past the field, the clouds parted, allowing bright shafts of sunlight to pierce through the sky and land as bright boxes of warm, shining light in the field. It was her. She was letting me know she was okay. My heart was calmed and I felt at peace.

Since that day, my grandmother has often made her presence known to me through light, or sudden shifts of light. She is always present in the penumbra of a candle, or in sun showers.

I still go to Rockport to watch the sunrise, because she is always in that first bluey glow of the brightening sky. I can smell the wool of her sweater and feel her arm around me. It is at times like these that I feel that she has stepped through the Thin Place, and death has no fetters.

Butterflies

Anne Heaton

When I was 21, I visited my grandmother Rosemary's grave at a cemetery filled with old oaks along the Illinois River. Rosemary had died in April of 1992 when I was 19, and I hadn't been to see her headstone since she was buried after the funeral mass. The grief I felt at my grandmother's passing is difficult to overstate. Since I was a little girl, I had dreaded her death, so much so that I frequently "rehearsed it," imagining what it would feel like to live without her. Rosemary was a heavy smoker, so perhaps this is why her death loomed in my

consciousness years before she did die of lung cancer. I'd hoped these test runs would lessen the blow. They did not.

I cherished my grandmother. I loved her graceful speech and quiet listening. She was a teacher and friend. She was an actual math and art elementary school teacher, and she was *my* teacher in that she showed me how to enjoy all the ordinary moments in a day: a free lollipop at the bank, smelling peonies, making dough. At her wake, previous students of hers in their 30's and 40's slipped in to say she had treated them with kindness. She was their favorite teacher.

Monarchs. Two, then three,
flying in little circles above me.
They didn't just pass through,
they stayed.

Rosemary was also wicked funny and she could laugh at herself with an Ernie giggle. "Oh, Anne," she'd say, "you're right." She never teased others though. Instead, she'd say, "What a good helper you are," "Aren't we good pals?" And about my parents, she'd say, "They're SUCH good kids."

A few days after her death, my father saw how distraught I was and said, "It will get easier in time." I said: "No. It will get harder in time. Now she is still close. We are talking about her, going to her funeral. Later, she will be far." Finally going to visit her grave that day was my way to get close to her.

I remember it was a sunny day. Perhaps it was summer. When I got to the cemetery, I found my way to her stone and sat down in front of it. I read her name: Rosemary Duffy Sinon. I cried and I lay on the ground. I had brought crayons, colored pencils, and paper. I don't know why. I guess I was going to journal or draw or see if she had any messages for me. What happened before I could do any of that, however, was that butterflies came. Monarchs. Two, then three, flying in little circles above me. They didn't just pass through, they stayed. They landed on her headstone, then resumed flying above it and my head, as I sat "criss-cross, apple-sauce." Then one of them landed on my arm and sat there as I looked at it. I'd never had a monarch land on me before. And I'd never had monarchs fly so closely around me for a significant amount of time. How long it was, I don't know. Ten minutes, maybe twenty minutes. I finally relaxed into the fact that they were staying with me, that my grandma was saying hello to me, remaining close.

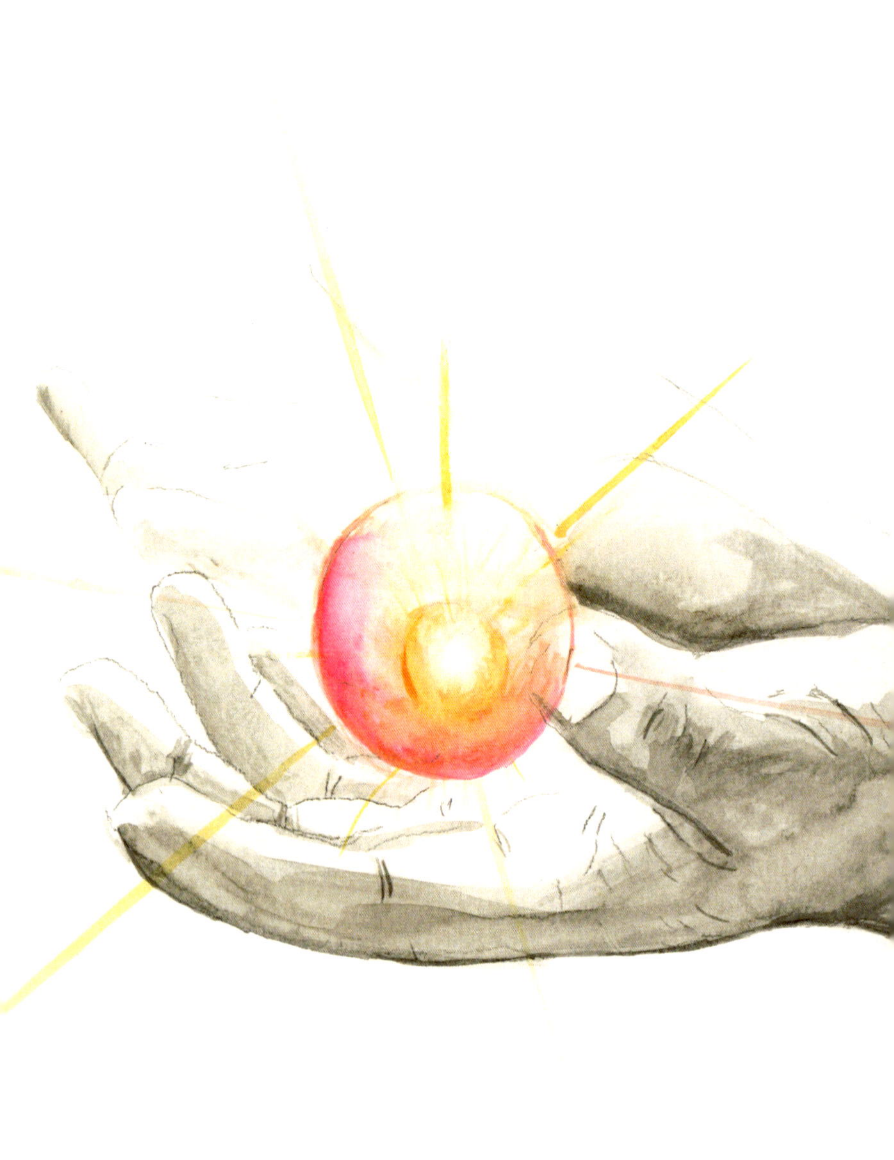

Energy

Emily Huber

Sometimes I experience an energy in my hands; they start to pulsate and get really hot. Often the feeling starts in my hands and travels through the rest of my body. When I was little this would happen, and I thought nothing of it. Once as a teenager, when that feeling came into my hands, I had a memory of my bubbe, Esther. I was sitting on her lap. She was holding my face in her hands, smiling as we looked into each other's eyes. She told me nothing was impossible. My Bubbe Esther and I were very close when I was little. I remember having really big belly laughs with her and lots of snuggles and tickle "fights." She and I shared a strong energetic connection.

My bubbe passed when I was four years old. My father told me that I was asleep in my bed and woke up suddenly, out-of-the-blue, screaming and crying. I wasn't sick, and my parents couldn't figure out what was wrong. The next morning, we found out that my Bubbe Esther had passed away.

I believe I felt her come to me before she left this world, and I can see how scary and sad that probably was for my four-year-old self. I imagine my heart was outside of my body watching her leave, and then returned to my body with so much pain as she departed this realm. I imagine my Bubbe Esther was saying goodbye. I didn't want her to go.

Hearing that story was an "aha" moment for me. I realized that I was, in fact, as connected to my grandmother as I thought. From then on, I knew that feeling in my hands was Bubbe Esther visiting me in the form of energy. It gave me such a thrill; I felt like I had a secret portal to another realm.

Now I welcome all her visits. It feels to me like a deep and powerful connection I'm so grateful for. She visits when I least expect it. Other times I ask her to join me. I started reaching out to her when I feel unbalanced or out of sorts. She comes, and her energy helps me recenter my being. As the years passed, I have invited her to join in some of my joys and celebrations. They always feel richer when I do. I love when she joins me in celebration as well as helping me through grief and pain.

Sometimes I reach out when I'm feeling fine just to feel her warm, gentle energy wrap around me like a soft blanket.

When I first started asking my grandmother to join me, I didn't know if I was making the whole thing up or if she was really there. The more I welcomed her though, the more I realized I was tapping into the universal force which included my Bubbe Esther. I feel so much love and gratitude for this connection. It's a reminder that she's always with me, through the very hard times and the very sweet times.

Bowl Full of Love

Margaret E. Ficarri-Ferraro

My nunna was a marvelous cook and fantastic baker. Her family immigrated to the United States from the Abruzzi region of Italy and she married my Calabrian grandfather when she was very young. During the holidays, as just about every day, her home was filled with the smell of delicious food and homemade Italian cookies. My earliest recollections are of times spent watching and being her kitchen assistant, learning how to cook and bake all the traditional Italian foods.

Along with homemade pasta, her Italian bread was a staple all year round. My grandmother would hand mix the dough in a huge aluminum mixing bowl.

While helping her, I learned all the secrets of making the perfect bread! When my nunna passed away, the mixing bowl was handed down to me.

I continued the Friday tradition of making dough for bread and pizzas for my family. My husband Joe and I were married for 46 years before he passed. Joe, also an Italian immigrant, enjoyed the tradition of making bread almost as much as he enjoyed eating it. Along with the smell of bread, he enjoyed hearing the music of what he would refer to as "the old country." I can still envision the dough rising in the bowl and hearing music, "*Con questo zeffiro, così soave,*" singing just above the clamor of our five children at play.

Just this past summer, I got a call from my great-granddaughters. To my delight, they wanted to learn "the secrets" of bread baking! So, every Wednesday this summer I pulled out that bowl and we made bread while I regaled them with stories of my grandmother, the 84-year-old mixing bowl, and Joe, their great-grandfather playing music from "the old country." At one point, the elder of the two great-granddaughters raised her hand and excitedly yelled, "Wait! Let's put on some Italian music!" Laughing as she located an Italian playlist, we waited. Then the song "*Santa Lucia*" played! I was overcome with emotion, as this was Joe's favorite song. I felt his presence there in the room with us celebrating this experience. As tears flowed, I was so happy. Of all the songs, this was his favorite.

Love endures and continues to express beyond form. The only question is, "Who gets the bowl?"

My earliest recollections
are of times spent watching
and being her kitchen assistant,
learning how to cook and bake
all the traditional Italian foods.

Oma's Apple Pie

Kira Simring

In Autumn of 2020, six months into the pandemic, I finally got to know my neighbors. I'd been living in a little suburb of Manhattan for five years and had made a point of staying mostly anonymous: go to work in New York City, raise a family in the suburbs of New Jersey. Keep it separate. A professional in the city, a mom in the burbs (and a wife and a daughter and a sister and an aunt and a cousin and a friend.) But then my neighbor, Reiko, brought me a homemade apple pie she'd lovingly baked with the apples she picked with her family at a nearby orchard. The crust was buttery, the apples tart and extra cinnamony. It was the first time I'd had apple pie like that since before the turn of the century when Oma, my maternal grandmother, was still alive.

And just like that, Oma was back.

When Oma died on September 19th of 1999, all the color drained from my world. I had cared for her the prior summer in her country home in Maryland, 75 minutes outside Washington, DC. "Nanjamoy" was a little farm with cows, a small apple orchard, fields of grass and hay, flowers everywhere, weeping willows, a forest of pine trees, and a wide creek surrounding. Although I was right there with her as she grew sicker and sicker, I could not accept that Oma was actually going to die. Afterwards, I would call her answering machine over and over again just to hear her singsong voice.

I finally felt reconnected to Oma when I had children. Like her, I struggled to balance the life of a professional artist with family obligations. She was a painter and a sculptor, as well as a world traveler, a music lover, an avid learner and a good friend. She was also the matriarch of our family. All of the grandchildren would fight over who got to sit next to Oma at family gatherings. (I fought the hardest and usually won.) She would always be sure to cut her homemade apple pies, stuffed with apples from her orchard, into perfectly even slices so none of us would throw a fit.

I told my mom about this ancestry project today and how very many years it took me to deal with losing Oma. She told me

she'd just had a dream about Oma the night before last, the same night I started this essay. In Mom's dream, she and I were with my daughter, Joji, when Oma just walked right in.

Oma was born in 1915. My daughter was born in 2015. It was only in writing this piece that I made the connection. An exact and entire matrilineal century.

Perfectly even slices.

Red Cardinal

Sarah Barab

Ever since I was a kid, my mom and I have had this joke. My mom would say, "No singing or laughing or dancing allowed!" at which point we would just sing and dance a lot more, laughing the entire time.

My mother loved birds. She knew the names, calls, and the song of every bird. Mom could even sing most of them, which was extraordinary. She loved many birds, but whenever a cardinal would come into her line of vision, she would release an excited gasp or scream: "Come here! Look at this cardinal!"

Since my mom's passing, there have been an unusual number of times when I have thought of my mom or am talking about my mom with a friend when suddenly a cardinal appears. It either flies past me or lands somewhere close to me. This has happened so many times it's beyond coincidence.

To be clear, I don't believe that *every* time I see a cardinal that it's literally my mother in the form of a bird. It's more the interconnectedness of my mother's love of birds, my love and connection to my mother, and then the auspicious timing of cardinals appearing as I think about her or talk about her. I'm not trying to make this logical. It doesn't even make sense to me.

Recently, a friend of mine was having a garage sale. I noticed a table with hand-woven bookmarks made in Nigeria. They were beautiful. "My mom would love this bookmark!" I commented. "If my mom were here, she would buy every single one of them to give as Christmas presents to friends." As I said this, my heart ached with longing for her. It's so hard to not be able to see her. A minute after I drove away from my friend's house, this cardinal flew directly in front of my windshield! Fortunately, I was far enough away not to hit it. As I slowed the car down, the cardinal landed on the road directly in front of my car. I was stunned. This beautiful cardinal stood there, simply looking at me. Without even thinking, I said, "Hi, mama." Suddenly, it flew off. As I wound my way back home, my heart felt deeply touched and a subtle peace came over me.

About a year ago, I was having an incredibly hard day. I decided to take a break and went to get some Thai food. I preferred to sit outside even though it was chilly. There was no place to sit, so I climbed onto a make-shift construction beam of sorts. Feeling bummed out and kind of depressed, I began to eat. I was missing both of my parents so much. Suddenly, a cardinal appeared on a telephone wire directly in front of me. To my astonishment, the cardinal began *dancing* for me, looking at me as it bounced up and down! It was also singing in my direction. This went on for at least five minutes. I kept wondering, "Is that bird really looking directly at me?" To my amazement, he just kept dancing, singing, and looking straight at me. It was so clear that it was my mom because her energy was there somehow.

I think that perhaps when we die, there's an ability to be many things at once. Do I believe that my mom is in the form of a bird? Not really. It's more that I think she is now *everywhere,* able to manifest in various ways. My hope is that my mother has reincarnated into another beautiful human being who has great parents and a wonderful life. But sometimes I know, especially when she comes to sing and dance with me, she's a cardinal.

Wheel of Fortune

Lisa Y. Ferraro

My maternal grandmother, Helen, and I share the same birthday. I would call to wish her a happy birthday, and with a sweet giggle she would respond, "Thank you. Same to you!"

Helen was a generous and loving presence in my life. She was the type of nunna who always had my back. We had a special bond.

Nunna always had a huge bag of toys in the corner of the living room. While the other children were playing with those, I could be found listening to "Moon River" which played from a music box made of tin. It was shaped like an old mill with a functional water wheel which served as the winding mechanism. It sparked my imagination and I simply couldn't get enough of it. When my nunna passed away, my mother knew that this music box should be handed down to me. Throughout the years I have prominently displayed this treasure on a bookcase or someplace similar. When I wind it and hear that song, it never fails to lift my spirits, launch my imagination and bring about a calm, joyful feeling.

...suddenly from the next room the music box began to play.

Several years after her passing, I came home from a long and disappointing work day. I was frustrated by all the "No's" I had received from my attempts to make a sale. As I sat lamenting my plight, suddenly from the next room the music box began to play. Not merely two or three stray notes, but it played "Moon River" from start to finish! I was startled because the box had not been wound for quite some time. I knew it was a sign from Helen, my grandmother, and I was left with a peace and presence knowing that all would be well.

The next morning, I felt a surge of optimism and rode a wave of enthusiasm to the office where I was one of the first representatives to arrive. I greeted my assistant and went back to begin lining up the calls for my day. No sooner had I arrived than a call was put through to me. The woman on the line wanted to place what was at that point the largest order I'd ever written. Her

name was Helen! That order alone put me well over my quota for the month. It was amazing. I just laughed and shook my head.

Late one afternoon a couple of weeks later, I was in the office working. As if to prove some cosmic point, I was once again the only sales associate there when a call came in for some assistance. Yet another woman named Helen who placed the largest order of my sales career. Everything shifted and I was well on my way. Thank you, Nunna!! I know you still have my back!

On another note, pun intended, I added the song, "Moon River" to my most recent jazz recording in honor of my nunna, Helen.

A Long-Distance Call

Terry Iacuzzo

Growing up in a family of psychics, it was expected that I would believe in all things paranormal without question. Is there really a world "beyond the veil"? I had questions. Many. I could never just believe what someone told me, even my own family. I *had* to experience it for myself. I wanted to know what was real.

I'm now 72 years old. One day I realized something: I didn't have anyone in my life who I was close to, who I had loved, who died. I had not known that kind of grief... not yet. Here's one of my stories of loss and love.

Jackie Brookner and I were partners in life for 25 years when cancer took her away 5 years ago. I was beyond lost. We had endless conversations about the meaning of life. She picked my brain every day about how I experienced visions, how I knew the things I did about the past, present, and future of a total stranger. What was the meaning of time? How did I experience that? Where do we go when we die? This drove me crazy, but she pushed me to think and articulate what being a psychic was. She encouraged me to savor every moment.

It was maybe six weeks after she died when I was abruptly awakened during the night. There she was at the end of my bed,

as clear as you are right now. She looked beautiful, radiant, and happy. I could barely breathe.

"Jackie, it's you!" I didn't want her to see how shaken I was. I wanted to touch her. I didn't want to cry. I knew this time would rush by. "Tell me, Jackie, what is it like there? Do you fly? Are you clairvoyant? Are you with your parents?" I felt ridiculous asking such questions but what I have learned from sitting in séance is that you keep talking to keep a spirit's attention held.

"Jackie, do you now know the answer to everything?"

"Terry, it's not like that."

For every question I asked, she repeated, "It's not like that." Then she showed me an enormous screen. My entire room was filled with images on the walls, the ceiling. I saw changing pictures of world apocalypses – floods, fires, buildings collapsing. Then just like that, it all stopped. Jackie moved her arm across the screen. "It's like this," she said.

I then had a feeling of extreme peace. I was filled with love. The curved screen (I can't say if it was blank or an empty space or prismatic colors) was filled with... the unseen. Clear, open, free... awareness. Just that.

After that night I started getting the phone calls. I didn't live with Jackie; I always had my own apartment. As she was an artist, she lived a few blocks from me in her studio loft. After we met and were together, I had installed a private telephone that only she had the number to. This way whenever it rang, I could answer it knowing it could only be her.

When she died, I didn't have the heart to disconnect it. Every night it rang at the very same time: 12:42am. Every night. The ring would be very quiet, just a few rings. It sounded like a quiet, shrill, little bird song. I'd stay awake and wait for it. I started feeling like it was Jackie calling me. But why at that time? Every night, same thing. Oh, yes, I'd jump up and catch the call and shout her name, begging for her to speak to me, but she never did.

One day, I had a thought. I wondered what time Jackie had died. I pulled out her death certificate. Yep, you guessed it: 12:42am.

This went on every night for many months. Then I got mad. I yelled at her to stop calling me at that hour, mostly because I was asleep! So, she changed the time. She now calls me at 10:31pm. Every night. What does that mean? Well, I was born on Halloween: October 31st… 10/31.

I miss her very much, but she calls me to say hello, I'm still here. One day, I know, I'll see her again.

Richard F. Floyd. FAII

January 27, 1997

Dearest Gary,

Enclosed you will find copies of three slides that we thought you might be able to use in same manner.

I know that you will write Amy a great letter and see that it is delivered to her personally, with out fail. You might also volunteer to appear on her show, open for her on the road and kiss her ass if necessary.

All my Love

Dad

The Letter

Gary Lynn Floyd

I thought my story was going to be about dragonflies, but it's not, so if there's a drawing of a dragonfly here, it's because I asked for it, and it's here for a reason: to remind me that I'm not alone.

This story is about a song. I remember driving to Nashville from Dallas on a certain road trip, and I heard a song called, "I'm Not Who I Was," by Brandon Heath. I literally pulled the car over to the side of the road and listened to the rest of the song. See, I had just lost my dad, and the song so beautifully expressed everything I felt about my relationship with him.

I get signs now and then from my dad, from the other dimension. A few days ago, I was clearing out another box from storage, and I found a framed photo and letter from my dad. It was a photo of me and a cardboard cutout of Amy Grant by my piano as a 17-year-old, and a letter from my dad, saying, "I know that you will write Amy a great letter and see that it is delivered to her personally without fail. You might also volunteer to appear on her show, open for her on the road and kiss her ass if necessary." This, coming from my dad, who's a Southern Baptist deacon. After a break in our relationship that seemed beyond repair, I had forgotten my dad had such a good sense of humor.

Fast forward to today. It just so happens that this Sunday I'm singing the song "I'm Not Who I Was" at a morning service and I'm sure that it's a sign from my dad that he gets me now, and that we're all good.

Oh, and every time I see a dragonfly, I know it's mom.

Ubiquitous

Kris Kollasch

The coffee pot gurgled and hissed as I stood at the kitchen sink, peering out into the backyard. I was thinking about the events of the weekend, the roller coaster of emotions that were about to ensue.

Saturday would be consumed by a passing and a party. The funeral was for a friend's mother who had recently died of cancer. I had never met the mom and our presence there was solely supportive. Even so, it would no doubt bring up emotions—thoughts of my own parental relationships or my partner's, who had been disowned by her own mother. Mother issues are never easy. Later that same evening we would join friends to celebrate July birthdays, mine included. The party would consist of dining and dancing to a Latin band at a fast-food Greek restaurant. Doing a little salsa at Opa, now that's a party!

Sunday would be the real heavy: a memorial service, a celebration of life for an old friend, Dr. Eileen Yellin. The "celebration" was to be held in the Tempe High School Auditorium. Even though it was the middle of summer, they opened it up for her and it would no doubt be full. Eileen had just retired as an English teacher and an advocate for at risk students. She was small in stature with a huge heart. Her soft, bubbly spirit guided her students and friends with kindness and generosity. Always giving of herself, she made the world a better place by inspiring the rest of us to be better humans. Having just turned 60, she finally retired and had plans to visit China with a friend and travel the world. She also had an ex-lover who suffered from mental illness.

My thoughts were on the phone call I had received a week earlier. I was away in Colorado, July 23rd, with my mother, visiting an old friend for breakfast. We were getting ready to head out for a walk on a beautiful summer day, noticing the birds and the loveliness of the day, when my cell phone rang. It was my partner who knew I had plans, so I felt like I needed to take the call. I was shocked and stunned when she told me Eileen Yellin had been killed, brutally murdered by her ex who then took her own life. So awful and tragic. So sudden and senseless and selfish.

All this rambled through my brain and sank into my heart as tears fell into the sink. The coffee pot let off its final pop and *sssissss* as it was ready to be pulled for the morning jolt I needed to start this day.

Then I heard it. "Ubiquitous."

I turned around and said out loud, "Ubiquitous?" in response. Someone had just spoken this to me over my right shoulder as clear as day. And I just repeated it, questioning this word I was sure I had never spoken before.

"Ubiquitous?" I did not really know what it meant. I had to look it up and repeat it to myself and understand it.

The Merriam-Webster dictionary defines "ubiquitous" (adjective) as: "existing or being everywhere at the same time; constantly encountered; widespread."

I believe Eileen spoke to me that day, out loud, clear and concise. One word was all she needed. After all, she was an English teacher. One word to tell me she was there, right here, right now... and everywhere.

Return to Roots: My Mom's Journey Home

Helen Yee

When I heard the news of my uncle's passing, I asked mom if she wanted me to accompany her to his funeral in Hong Kong. She replied that she wanted my youngest brother, Henry, to make this trip with her as it could help shake him from a challenging time in his young life. Mom was extremely worried about him. As my niece Shelly and I took mom to the airport, she expressed concern that Henry would not follow up on getting his US passport. She was also worried none of her kids would burn incense at the ancestor temple in Kowloon if/when she died. Shelly and I tried to console her, but she seemed very distraught. All I could say to her was, "Oh, mom, don't talk that way."

After she boarded the plane, Shelly turned to me and said, "Grandma did not bring any of her medication with her." Shelly also noticed that Mom hadn't gone to the hairdresser before she left. This was highly unusual for my mom who was impeccable when it came to her appearance. As Mom predicted, Henry did not get his passport, so did not make the trip to meet her in Hong Kong.

On the day of my uncle's funeral, I received a call from my cousin Larry in Hong Kong. He was concerned about mom who was talking and not making any sense. I told him to get her to the hospital as it sounded like symptoms of a stroke. I booked myself on the next flight from the US to Hong Kong. Once there, I was greeted by my cousins, aunt, and uncle. My aunt looked at me and said, "You're late." I replied that I thought my flight had arrived on time. She said, "No, I didn't mean the plane. It's your mom. You're too late. She has passed away." They'd notified my partner Diane and she was en route as well.

I was palpably feeling my mother's presence as I allowed myself to also fully feel my emotions. As we approached the next stop, I knew without a doubt the essence of my mother was with me, guiding us along the way.

My mom's passing coincided with the celebration of the end of Hong Kong's 100 year lease to the British. Hong Kong was being returned back to China. Now my own mother was also returning back to China.

The next two weeks were spent tending to my uncle's estate and arranging mom's funeral. One day, my other uncle asked whether we would like to see the largest Buddha in Hong Kong or the new airport. He seemed very excited about the new airport, so we agreed to tour the new airport.

While returning from the airport tour, our guide wanted to stop where ancient villages called Hutongs were located. As we were walking through them, I noticed huge black-and-white photos of three women hanging above an altar. As our guide shared the history of the Hutong in Cantonese, my uncle got very excited. He realized this Hutong belonged to the family of Tsang, which is my mom's maiden name. My uncle said that this Hutong was the village of Tsang and had belonged to my ancestors at one time. He said the women in those photos above the altar were my ancestors. Still emotional and a bit shocked at the Hutong revelation, I heard our guide suggest one final and random stop. I was palpably feeling my mother's presence as I allowed myself to also fully feel my emotions. As we approached the next stop, I knew without a doubt the essence of my mother was with me, guiding us along the way. The tour guide brought us to the front of the ancestor temple.

I recalled the words of concern my mother spoke aloud weeks prior on the way to the airport. In my heart, I knew my opportunity to burn incense for my mom, uncle, and all of my ancestors was guided by an unseen force: all of my relatives in the afterlife. My mother's final wishes were granted.

A few months before my mother died, my partner Diane and I attended an event which hosted a psychic who was doing short readings for the audience. He looked straight at me and said, "You are going to learn much about your ancestors and heritage this year." As we were leaving, I said to Diane that that would never happen because I was not planning on returning to Hong Kong. How little we knew.

I am appreciative of all that unfolded on this journey and for my mom's return home.

My Father and the Great Blue Heron

Eugenia Zukerman

The first time I saw that beautiful blue bird I was simply looking into a stream near the road. Intrigued, I moved toward it and felt its bright blue eyes lock onto mine... or was I imagining it?

I moved carefully closer and the bird tilted its head, summoning me to come to him. Wearing rubber boots, I moved toward the bird and it suddenly took off but circled back, as if wondering what kind of creature I might be. That evening I dreamed about the encounter. When I woke up in the morning, I felt particularly content.

Some weeks later, I travelled to Washington DC to perform at the Kennedy Center. I was really nervous, so I decided to take a nap the afternoon of the concert. As I put my head on the pillow, I closed my eyes and sensed something hovering, almost fluttering near my head. My eyes were closed but it made me feel safe, and when I woke up I felt particularly strong and energetic.

Since that first encounter by the road, I've often walked past the stream, and without fail, I have seen that gorgeous blue heron. Is it the same one? Is it a mirage?

Soon after those walks, I attended the wedding of a niece, and as the ceremony came to its end, a great blue heron circled above the bride and groom.

Was the bird wanting some wedding cake? Or was it a relative of the great blue heron who had decided to adopt our family?

I loved my father, but he was demanding. His expectations were difficult to live up to. In fact, just writing about him makes me tingle with a degree of fear.

But I often dream of him and imagine him tucked into the reeds, staring up at me with his bright blue eyes.

Garter Snakes

Andrea Elliott

One of my most distinct memories from childhood is when a boy in my third-grade class told me he was selling garter snakes for fifty cents. I couldn't believe my good luck. It was an unexpected opportunity and I took him up on the offer immediately. I would take one for fifty cents. Absolutely. He showed up that night, thankfully interrupting a dinner of spaghetti which I didn't like, with the novel creature. I got a fifty-cent piece from my wooden house bank and he handed over the snake, which I named Sneaky Joe (after my Grandpa Joe).

I had this snake for about a year. It was my constant companion. Very pacific, I often carried him about around my neck. So, it subsequently made sense that my sister would show up as garter snakes the summer after she died on May 1st, 2019. I always hope to see snakes in the yard, but I don't really see many, or any, very often.

However, I saw many garter snakes in the summer of 2020. I saw several in the yard, and a couple in Hudson. They were showing up that summer. I even saw a teeny tiny baby one. One day, I found one that was delightfully tame. It gave me no trouble in picking it up. I played with it for quite a while, eventually placing it on a banana plant whereupon I captured several photographs.

It's now the summer of 2021, and I don't think I've seen a snake in the yard this summer at all. Last year, 2020, was the summer of the garter snake. That's when Jackie was showing up and letting me know she was there.

My Mom's Coat

Safiya Randera

Early in the pandemic, I went to visit dad. When I was leaving, he insisted I take your jacket. It wasn't cold out. He said, "It's your mom's. Take it so you'll remember her."

I resisted at first because, to be honest, it wasn't my style. It's not that it's ugly (you always had great taste) but you know how picky I can be. Also, the idea that I needed a jacket to remember you seemed so ridiculous to me, although I do keep a pair of your old slippers (the ones with the pink ribbons on them) in the corner of my room.

But you know that already.

Anyway, I ended up taking it just to make him happy. A few weeks later I put it on to take Owen out for a walk… and I felt like you were hugging me. That super soft, cozy lining and the weight of it on my body was so incredibly soothing for my nervous system.

We are always connecting through the ether. You watch over me, guide me, and protect me. But I was going on months without touch.

Somehow you knew that what I really needed was a hug.

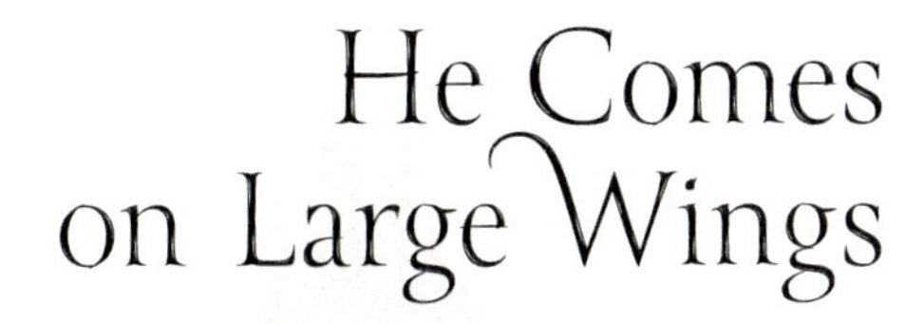

He Comes on Large Wings

Allen Angel

My dad's nickname was Tombstone or Tomb for short, a moniker given to him by his male buddies. He was self-employed for 55 years, selling monuments along with grave spaces from the two cemeteries the business owned.

A sense of humor was very important to my dad. He came equipped with a good one, as well as strong joke-telling skills. He liked to tease me as he did everyone he had an affection for. In time, I learned to return his teasing. That give and take was always a big part of our relationship.

Although we never talked of nature, wildlife, or went on hikes, my dad saw the beauty, value, and importance of nature. I adopted the same tenets. His communication and sharing of that ideology came and still comes on large wings in numerous shapes, colors, and sizes, in different circumstances and in various environments.

Large birds, specifically vultures, turkeys (some albino), an occasional owl, and lots of hawks have always seemed to appear on my radar. Some would say it's just happenstance, but it has occurred too often for me to believe there isn't more to the story. It's taken me a while to figure it out. I've come to the conclusion they are "visits" from my dad. It feels like he's just checking in with me, letting me know I'm still in his thoughts.

My first large bird visit happened within the city limits of Madison, WI, in a small wooded area adjacent to a crop field on one side and a congested development on the other. It was my first time at this house. I just happened to be looking out the window when I saw an owl fly in the opposite direction, then reappear at the edge of the woods, talons securing a rabbit on the ground.

Another big bird visit occurred when I rented a secluded cabin with a steep driveway and a heavily wooded area in the rear. It rained for two or three days, and on the first rainy day I noticed something black in a small cluster of tall pines. A bit of a mystery, I was eager to find out what it was. The steep incline and continuous rain presented obstacles, but I had binoculars in the car which allowed for a closer look. There were four turkey vultures huddled up, keeping themselves warm, and using the pine boughs to stay dry. They remained huddled through the rains, and I'd check on them each morning and evening. When the weather cleared, they were off for thermals. I felt so lucky to have a front row seat!

One summer, I was house-sitting along a switchback road heading up a mountain gap. As the terrain flattened out, I spotted two large trees that served as roosts for wild turkeys every night. There were 15-25 albino turkeys! They would be visible in the trees prior to the morning warm up or in the evening before sunset. On foggy mornings, they would still be roosting, looking like hefty leaf collections. At least twice a day, they would cross the road. They're amazingly quick. After entering woods and ground cover, they disappear until suddenly they aren't visible at all. On this morning, there were six of them with a variety of colors: white, dark, and some in between. They crossed the road, entered the woods, and were gone. No noise, no vegetation moving, no nothing. Seeing them for several days was quite a treat!

I can only hope the "visits" continue for years to come.

My Heron or Yours

Natalía Zukerman

The Soul of my grandfather lives on in a bird
That's what my mother said
Now this from the most practical of women
In the most practical dress
"The Last Few Miles," by Natalia Zukerman

A few years after my grandfather died, my mother announced that she thought his spirit lived on in a great blue heron. I remember being surprised and excited by this proclamation because I hadn't been aware of my mom's spiritual beliefs prior to this statement. She explained that it was an overwhelming feeling she had, and that the bird appeared at auspicious moments to let her know he was there. At my cousin's wedding, just at the moment of their vows, an enormous heron flew past the couple. Everyone gathered ooh-ed and ahh-ed.

I lived in Newburport, MA, for a few years, a little Rockwellian village north of Boston, near a bird sanctuary and thousands of miles of protected seashore. I moved there to be with my girlfriend at the time. The relationship was a difficult and fraught one. I often found myself wandering alone in the marshes and paths that skirted the ocean. Herons would sometimes show up, appearing with a great swoosh of wings, a dramatic gravity defying lift off, impossibly curved neck, and prehistoric wingspan. Or sometimes, there would simply be one quietly standing among the reeds, watching me as I watched it. Was it my grandfather coming to be with me, to tell me that this relationship wasn't right for me? Or was it simply a clue to check in with myself, to tap into the truth that I already knew? The day I finally packed up and drove away from that town for the last time, a giant heron swooped down in front of my car, almost too close to my windshield.

My grandfather was a brilliant man; an inventor and scientist who told the most wonderful bedtime stories to me and my sister. There were stories of time travel, shape shifting, solar powered flying cars, and probably most "famously" (within my family lore only of course) the one about the "pooping bunny" who was able to propel his own flight by flapping his enormous ears and leaving his signature markings on his makeshift runways. The adults didn't love his scatological humor, but all the grandkids delighted in every off-color joke and wild story.

My mother is now in cognitive decline. I moved nearby to be closer to her, to help as her disease progresses and to spend as much time with her as I can. Her dementia has been beautiful and painful. In its best teaching moments, it has reminded and

highlighted how time and existence are on a continuum. We walk together at least once a week and I note how she often tells the same story at exactly the same part of our walk. Perhaps a color, a smell, or a sound will ignite part of her memory. Or maybe it's about timing and the rhythm of our steps. She is a musician after all. It's almost as if there's a score, alerting her like, "This is the measure and beat where I now tell the story about the forsythia and the couple I knew in London when I was first married to your father." I delight in noticing and am gathering practices that keep us both rooted in the present as the past parades by.

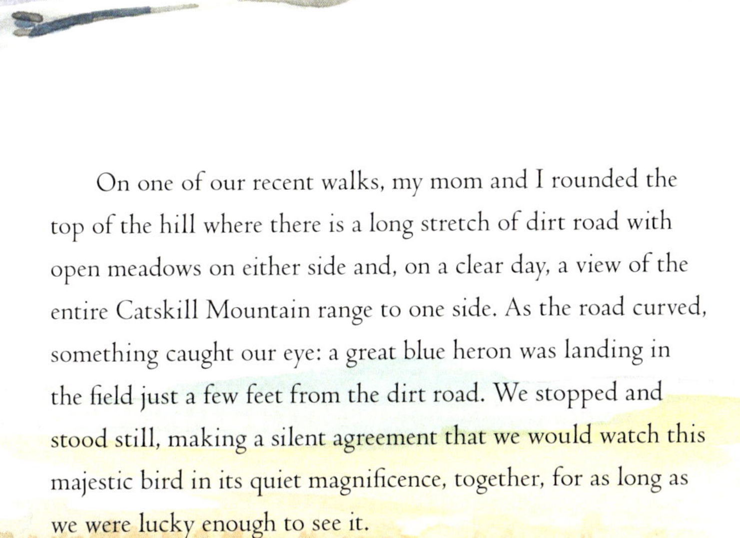

On one of our recent walks, my mom and I rounded the top of the hill where there is a long stretch of dirt road with open meadows on either side and, on a clear day, a view of the entire Catskill Mountain range to one side. As the road curved, something caught our eye: a great blue heron was landing in the field just a few feet from the dirt road. We stopped and stood still, making a silent agreement that we would watch this majestic bird in its quiet magnificence, together, for as long as we were lucky enough to see it.

I was learning to recognize
the presence of spirit.

Out of the Blue

Maí Bloomfield

For the first few days after my mom passed, I moved about in her empty house in a slow daze. My brain struggled to make sense of her sudden disappearing act. The day-planner on her desk was full of her to-do's, the blue post-it note with my handwritten "good morning mom!" clung to the kitchen cupboard, and her small, fuzzy slippers were waiting at the foot of the bed. Even though I'd been through cancer myself, and her cancer had been around for a while, nothing could have prepared me for it.

My heart ached in unfamiliar ways, as if walls had fallen away and it was looking for something to hold on to. It also felt strangely open. I felt like my mom's presence and my love for her were expanding, like something inside me, and all around me was stretching out, blooming, opening up like a giant umbrella. One morning, I sat outside in her big patio chair, quiet with the winter sun on my face. Out of nowhere, a scuffle erupted at the back of my neck. Something flurried close to my cheek. I jolted, then froze. I turned my head slowly, daring to get a better view. There, beside my shoulder, on the rim of the armchair, a beautiful blue jay appeared. Inches from my nose, the bird cocked its indigo head side to side, inspecting me. We stared gently at one another for several minutes and I began to cry.

In that delicate space, I felt the immediacy of my mom's spirit. I felt our love for each other. I breathed it in, watching the pretty bird puff up its blue-grey chest. It wasn't that I thought my mother was the bird, exactly. I just felt this divine closeness to something that seemed untouchable, otherworldly. It was as if a veil had lifted, and in the space between us there was a simple, quiet confirmation: *We are connected*. Even that which flies toward heaven can connect with those who remain on the ground. In a heartbeat, the big invisible "somewhere out there" landed right in my lap.

More than a sign, my encounter with the blue jay felt like an opening. I was learning to recognize the presence of spirit. For spirit, just like love, is invisible, isn't it? How do you know when love is there? You experience it, you feel it, and then you just know. When I am present to the love I share with my mom, I feel my mom's spirit, present in the love. The bird was an invitation. It's astonishing proximity provided the jolt my body needed to register the revelation: *We are connected to the ones we love, always. Even when they are no longer here.*

The blue jay stayed for a while. Then it disappeared. I must've turned my head, because I didn't see it take flight. But when I looked down, I found a slender blue feather, resting at my feet.

Contributors

Allen Angel Reader. Observer of nature.

Amber Darland Singer-songwriter. Teacher. Parent. Creative. amberdarland.com

Andrea Elliott Acupuncturist/Chinese Herbal Medicine Specialist. Rainforest Enthusiast. Chinese Speaker. elliottacupuncture.net

Anne Heaton Healing Humor & Happiness Soul Song Maker. Coffee Drinker. anneheaton.com

Billie Gray Educational Consultant. Grief Coach. Mentor.

Bob Weisenburger Lipetz Life enthusiast. Word Whisperer.

Carolyn Gerdeman Seeker. Music Lover. Singer. Gigi. Integral part of Universe.

Rev. Christie Hardwick Spirit evangelist. Author. Singer. Songwriter. Gmama. Adventurer. inspirationgatherings.org

Deirdre Michael Urban planner. Musician. Rabbit hole enthusiast.

Dominique Sacco Jesus follower. Wife. Mother. Animal lover

Emily Huber Health and wellness practitioner. Teacher. Lover to all. bodybrainbalance.me

Eugenia Zukerman Flutist. Writer. Television commentator. Mom. GrammE. Lover of long walks. eugeniazukerman.com

Gary Lynn Floyd Singer. Songwriter. Artist. Human. Being. garylynnfloyd.com

Kate Mapother Writer. Poet. Instagram: @brightenuff

Kira Simring Mama. Artist. Director. thecelltheatre.org

Kris Kollasch Artist. Designer. Curator. Animal Lover. Believer in Miracles. artandenvironments.com

Mai Bloomfield Writer. Musician. Singer. Artist. Explorer. Francophile. Foodie. Nature-Lover. maibloomfield.com

Margaret Ficarri-Ferraro Mother. Nunny. Baker. Cook. Homemaker.

Marie Martini Healer. Wonder seeker. Intuitive. Curious mind. Spontaneous spirit. mariemartini.amtamembers.com

Safiya Randera Artist. Wizard. heartofearth.ca/about

Sarah Barab Holistic astrologer. Somatic therapist. Filmmaker. Buddhist. Friend. sarahbarab.com

Sifu Helen Yee Teacher of internal energy systems: Chigong and Tai Chi Master. aiam.edu

Terry Iacuzzo Psychic. Tarot scholar. Golden Heart. Saint. terryiacuzzo.com

Editorial assistance provided by Daniel Dyer and Greg Adair.